Y0-BYZ-091

Frederick Douglass

JOSH GREGORY

Children's Press®
An Imprint of Scholastic Inc.

Content Consultant
James Marten, PhD
Professor and Chair, History Department
Marquette University
Milwaukee, Wisconsin

Library of Congress Cataloging-in-Publication Data
Gregory, Josh.
  Frederick Douglass / Josh Gregory.
    pages cm. — (A true book)
  Includes bibliographical references and index.

  ISBN 978-0-531-21597-5 (library binding : alk. paper) — ISBN 978-0-531-21759-7 (pbk. : alk. paper)
  1. Douglass, Frederick, 1818–1895—Juvenile literature. 2. Abolitionists—United States—Biography—Juvenile literature. 3. African American abolitionists—Biography—Juvenile literature. 4. Antislavery movements—United States—Juvenile literature. I. Title.
  E449.D75G74 2015
  973.8092—dc23 [B]   2014044840

© 2016 Scholastic Inc.
All rights reserved. Published in 2016 by Children's Press, an imprint of Scholastic Inc. Published simultaneously in Canada. Printed in China 62
SCHOLASTIC, CHILDREN'S PRESS, A TRUE BOOK™, and associated logos are trademarks and/or registered trademarks of Scholastic Inc.
1 2 3 4 5 6 7 8 9 10 R 25 24 23 22 21 20 19 18 17 16

Front cover: Portrait of Frederick Douglass

Back cover: Title page from the first edition of Douglass's autobiography

Find the Truth!

Everything you are about to read is true *except* for one of the sentences on this page.

Which one is **TRUE**?

T or F   Frederick Douglass was the first African American to hold a high position in the U.S. government.

T or F   Frederick Douglass's grandmother taught him how to read.

Find the answers in this book.

Contents

1 Born into Slavery

What difficulties did Frederick Douglass
face as a child?............................. 7

2 Making an Escape

How did Douglass free himself from slavery? 17

3 Spreading a Message

Why did Douglass travel to Europe after
publishing his autobiography?................ 27

**Sojourner
Truth**

THE BIG TRUTH!

The Abolitionist Movement

Who joined Douglass in the battle
to end slavery?..................... 34

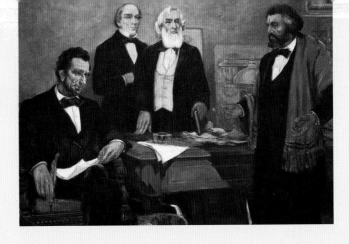

Douglass (right) meets with President Abraham Lincoln (left) during the Civil War.

4 A National Leader

How did Douglass continue fighting injustice after slavery was abolished? **37**

True Statistics........... **44**

Resources **45**

Important Words........ **46**

Index **47**

About the Author........ **48**

Douglass's newspaper, The North Star, had about 4,000 subscribers throughout the world.

Frederick Douglass escaped from slavery and helped end it by sharing his remarkable story with the public.

CHAPTER 1

Born into Slavery

The United States is often called the land of the free. Yet for much of the country's early history, African Americans were held as slaves. Captured from their homes in Africa and sold to work in America, they and their descendants were considered property. As property, they had no freedom. Eventually, however, brave **activists** began calling for an end to slavery. Among them was a former slave named Frederick Douglass.

Frederick Douglass's home in Washington, D.C., is now a National Historic Site.

An Uncertain Birthdate

Douglass was born Frederick Augustus Washington Bailey on a **plantation** in Maryland sometime around 1817 or 1818. Like many enslaved people, he was never sure of his exact birthdate. Slave owners purposely kept such information from their slaves. Frederick could only roughly guess his age after overhearing his owner mention that he was about 17 years old in 1835.

Plantations were sprawling farms that relied almost entirely on slave labor to operate.

Slave children were often taken from their parents and placed in the care of older slaves.

Frederick's mother was a slave named Harriet Bailey. He was not sure who his father was. However, he heard rumors that his father was his mother's white owner, a man called Captain Anthony.

When he was still a baby, Frederick was taken from his mother. He was sent to live with his grandmother, who was also a slave. Because Harriet lived several miles away and worked all day, Frederick rarely saw her. She died when he was about seven years old.

Slave homes lacked even the most basic comforts.

Plantation Life

Almost all African slaves in the United States were forced to live in very poor conditions. Most slaves lived and worked in the southern states. Many, like Frederick, worked on large plantations. On these huge farms, slaves often lived in very simple huts or cabins. Frederick was no exception. Instead of beds, slaves on Frederick's plantation slept on cold, damp floors and had coarse blankets.

The slaves' food was filling but not enough to keep them healthy. Frederick and the other children were given cornmeal mush in a shared **trough**. They didn't have spoons. Instead, they scooped up the food using objects such as seashells or shingles.

Sometimes, white overseers punished slaves with beatings or whippings. These punishments could be brutal. At times, slaves died from their injuries. Young Frederick saw all of this happen.

Striking a slave with a long whip was a common form of punishment on plantations.

11

Off to Baltimore

In 1826, Frederick was sent to Baltimore to work for Hugh Auld, a ship carpenter and a relative of his owner. There, he took care of Auld's son, Thomas, and helped Auld with his work. Living in the city was a big change for Frederick. He lived in Auld's home, where he slept in a real bed. He also had plenty to eat. However, he was still far from free.

Slaves who worked in their masters' homes often lived more comfortable lives than those who worked outdoors.

Learning to read put Frederick on the path to becoming a skilled writer and public speaker.

Learning to Read

Auld's wife, Sophia, treated Frederick very kindly at first. She was not used to having slaves, and she saw him as a person instead of property. As a result, she gave him something that was even better than a warm bed and a good meal. She began teaching him how to read. This changed Frederick's life forever.

Education was extremely rare for slave children.

A Lasting Lesson

When Auld found out that his wife was teaching Frederick to read, he was very angry. He told her to stop the lessons. It was illegal in slave states to teach a slave to read. Knowing how to read and write would make it easier for slaves to communicate and to acquire information. A black person who could write might create fake official documents that could help a slave escape.

Continuing Education

Sophia stopped teaching Frederick and, over time, began to treat him more cruelly. However, Frederick did everything he could to keep learning on his own. He secretly read books and newspapers whenever possible. He sometimes sneaked a look at the schoolbooks of the Aulds' young son when no one was around. He also made friends with poor white children in the neighborhood. They helped him practice writing.

Frederick found friends in the streets of Baltimore who helped him learn to write.

Leaving Baltimore meant that Frederick had to start working as a field laborer.

CHAPTER 2

Making an Escape

While Frederick was in Baltimore, his original master, Captain Anthony, died. Ownership of Frederick was passed to Anthony's son-in-law, Thomas Auld. Though Frederick continued to work for Hugh, he was Thomas's property. Then in 1832, Thomas and Hugh had an argument. To punish Hugh, Thomas took Frederick to live with him. Unlike Hugh, Thomas often beat and starved his slaves. Frederick stood up to these cruel actions by disobeying orders.

In 1830, more than two million people in the United States were slaves.

Fighting Back

Thomas decided to send Frederick to a man named Edward Covey. Covey was famous in the area for using violence to "break" slaves and make them obedient. For several months, Covey forced Frederick to work long hours doing hard physical labor in all weather conditions. He beat Frederick often, sometimes for no reason at all.

Slave breakers like Edward Covey kept a close watch over workers and did not hesitate to use violence.

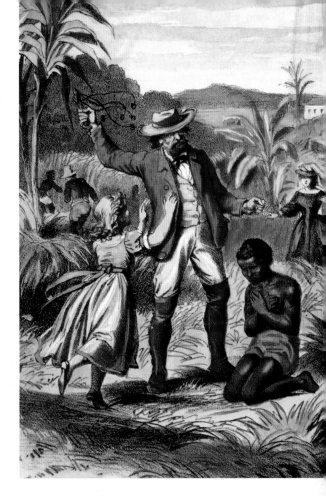

Fighting back against a master was dangerous. A slave risked an even more severe punishment.

At first, Frederick became **depressed** by the situation. But one day, he suddenly found the strength to resist. When Covey tried to beat him, Frederick fought back. Covey called for help from the other slaves, but they refused. After a two-hour struggle, Frederick had made it clear he wouldn't give in. Covey could not defeat Frederick himself and was too embarrassed to have him whipped publicly. The man never hit Frederick again.

Frederick did his best to share knowledge with as many fellow slaves as possible.

Frederick later wrote that his Sunday lessons were "the sweetest engagement with which I was ever blessed."

Sunday School

In 1834, Frederick was sent to live with yet another master, William Freeland. Freeland treated Frederick far better than Thomas Auld had. Frederick quickly made friends with Freeland's two other slaves. When they found out he could read, they asked him to teach them. He began holding secret classes on Sundays. Slaves came from plantations all around the area to learn from Frederick.

Escape Plans

Eventually, Frederick and his friends began working on a plan to escape. They knew that slavery was illegal in the northern states and that people there would help them hide. They decided to steal a canoe and travel north by water. However, word of their plan reached their owners. Frederick and his friends were caught on the day they planned to leave.

Escaped slaves faced difficult journeys as they made their way north.

Another Try

Frederick was separated from his friends and sent back to Hugh Auld in Baltimore. There, he worked at the city's docks, learning to build and repair ships. In September 1838, he decided to try escaping once again. He obtained false identification that said he was a **freedman** and disguised himself as a sailor. Then he got on a train heading north.

Frederick was sometimes harassed by white workers as he worked at Baltimore's docks.

22

Anna Murray

While working at the Baltimore docks, Frederick met a woman named Anna Murray. Born free to former slaves, Anna earned money by doing laundry for ship captains. Frederick and Anna soon fell in love. She encouraged him to seek his freedom. She even provided him with some money and the sailor's uniform he used to escape in 1838.

As he made his way north, Frederick was terrified that he would be captured.

The Home Stretch

Less than a day after leaving Baltimore, Frederick arrived in New York City. He had little money and nowhere to live. He was scared that his owners would track him down. However, he soon met a man who would help—an **abolitionist** named David Ruggles. Ruggles was a free black man who helped slaves escape to freedom. He took Frederick to a safe house to hide.

New Home, New Name

Frederick sent word to Anna that he had reached New York. She joined him there, and they were soon married. Frederick and Ruggles decided it would be best for the couple to move to New Bedford, Massachusetts. There, Frederick could find a job working with ships. Ruggles gave the newlyweds some money and helped them reach their new home. They took the last name Douglass. This would make it harder for Frederick's former owners to find him.

New York City was home to helpful abolitionists, but it was also one of the first places a plantation owner might look for escaped slaves.

The Douglasses arrive in New Bedford.

26

CHAPTER 3

Spreading a Message

In Massachusetts, Douglass began to build a new life with Anna. They soon started a family, eventually having five children. To support them, Douglass worked a variety of odd jobs. It was sometimes difficult to find work. Even though slavery was illegal in the North, black people living there were still not always treated fairly. Many white people would not hire them for jobs.

New Bedford was settled by European colonists in 1652.

Joining the Movement

As a free man, Douglass was able to read whatever he wanted, whenever he wanted. He began subscribing to abolitionist newspapers. In them, he read about the ways people were working to end slavery completely. He also started attending local abolitionist meetings, where people shared their ideas for ways to help.

Abolitionist meetings such as this gathering in London, England, often drew both black and white supporters.

William Lloyd Garrison founded the New England Anti-Slavery Society in 1832.

At these meetings, Douglass became friends with important abolitionist leaders such as William Lloyd Garrison. They wanted Douglass to share his story with others. At first, he was unsure. He did not want to draw too much attention to himself. But one day in 1841, he stood up and spoke to a crowd in the town of Nantucket. The audience was awed by his remarkable tale and his impressive way with words.

Police and pro-slavery whites break up an abolitionist meeting as Douglass delivers a speech.

Speaking Out

Douglass was still afraid of being caught. However, he knew that his life story and speaking skills could help spread the abolitionist cause. He toured the northern states, giving speeches about his experiences as a slave. He became famous for his passionate arguments against slavery. Though he was sometimes met with harsh treatment from pro-slavery whites, he never gave up.

Sharing His Story

In 1845, Frederick published the first of his three **autobiographies**. The book became a best seller. In it, Douglass included detailed descriptions of the violence and mistreatment he had experienced while a slave. The book was the first time many readers were exposed to the true horrors of slavery.

Narrative of the Life of Frederick Douglass became a best seller and made Douglass famous.

NARRATIVE

OF THE

LIFE

OF

FREDERICK DOUGLASS,

AN

AMERICAN SLAVE.

WRITTEN BY HIMSELF.

BOSTON:

PUBLISHED AT THE ANTI-SLAVERY OFFICE,

No. 25 CORNHILL.

1846.

Traveling Abroad

Because he included the names of his former owners in his book, Douglass was more afraid than ever that they would find him. To avoid being captured, he traveled to Europe. There, he continued giving speeches and gathering support for the effort to end slavery. He made many friends and was amazed at how well people treated him overseas.

Abolitionists in Europe did everything they could to support Douglass after hearing his story.

After returning home, Douglass went right back to work spreading his message about the evils of slavery.

Finally Free

Though he was successful in Europe, Douglass knew he needed to return home. He wanted to be with his family and continue fighting to end slavery. To help, his European supporters raised the money he needed to pay his former owners for his freedom. This made him legally free. An escaped slave could be captured and returned to slavery. A free person could not. In 1847, he returned home, able to speak and write without fear.

The Abolitionist Movement

Frederick Douglass was only one of many people working to end slavery in the United States. From the earliest days of the nation, people spoke out against this horrible practice. Here are some of the most famous of them.

William Lloyd Garrison
An early supporter of Douglass, William Lloyd Garrison began publishing the antislavery newspaper *The Liberator* in 1831. Garrison was known for his controversial political opinions. While many abolitionists argued only for slaves' freedom, Garrison also argued for equality for African Americans.

Harriet Tubman

After escaping slavery when she was about 29 years old, Harriet Tubman dedicated herself to helping others do the same on the Underground Railroad. Slave owners offered rewards for her capture, while abolitionists praised her heroic deeds.

Sojourner Truth

Like Frederick Douglass, Sojourner Truth was a former slave who became famous for her powerful antislavery speeches. Later in life, she dedicated herself to the cause of women's rights and provided advice to recently freed slaves.

John Brown

Unlike most abolitionists, John Brown believed that violence was the only way to end slavery. In October 1859, he and an armed group of followers took about 60 people hostage in Harpers Ferry, Virginia, which is now part of West Virginia. Brown hoped to inspire slaves to join him in rebellion. However, his plan was unsuccessful. He was convicted of treason, or betraying the country, and hanged.

CHAPTER 4

A National Leader

After returning to the United States, Douglass decided to start his own abolitionist newspaper. Called *The North Star*, its first issue was published on December 3, 1847. Unlike other similar newspapers, it was owned, written, and edited by African Americans. It included everything from news articles to poems and book reviews. Douglass himself wrote many of the paper's articles.

Subscriptions to *The North Star* cost two dollars per year.

The North Star was named for the bright star in the night sky that escaped slaves used as a guide toward freedom.

Douglass was the only African American to attend the first women's rights convention in 1848.

Freedom and Equality for All

In addition to wanting to end slavery, Douglass believed in equality for all Americans. In *The North Star*, his other writings, and his speeches, he often discussed the importance of equal rights for women. He also wrote often about the necessity of education for all Americans.

A Spectacular Speech

On July 5, 1852, Frederick Douglass delivered one of the best-known speeches of his career. He spoke at a Fourth of July celebration in Rochester, New York. In front of a crowd of about 500 people, he pointed out that Independence Day did not mark freedom for African Americans. It only stood for the freedom of the nation's white residents. He called for the country to embrace its founding principles of freedom and equality by ending slavery.

The End of Slavery

In the 1850s, the national debate over slavery became more and more heated. Many people in the northern states wanted abolition. However, plantation owners in the southern states did not want to give up their source of free labor. Finally, the Civil War broke out between the North and the South in 1861. Douglass hoped that the conflict could bring an end to slavery once and for all.

Timeline of Fredrick Douglass's Life

1817–1818
Frederick Augustus Washington Bailey is born on a plantation in Maryland.

1838
Frederick escapes from slavery and takes the last name Douglass.

During the Civil War, Douglass encouraged free black men to join the military and fight against the South. He even met with President Abraham Lincoln to discuss the way black soldiers were treated. He wanted to make sure they received fair payment for their services.

The North defeated the South in 1865. Later that year, Congress approved the 13th **Amendment** to the U.S. Constitution, which officially ended slavery throughout the country.

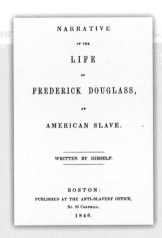

NARRATIVE

OF THE

LIFE

OF

FREDERICK DOUGLASS,

AN

AMERICAN SLAVE.

WRITTEN BY HIMSELF.

BOSTON:
PUBLISHED AT THE ANTI-SLAVERY OFFICE,
No. 25 CORNHILL.
1846.

1865
The 13th Amendment abolishes slavery in the United States.

1845
Douglass publishes his first autobiography and travels to Europe.

More to Do

Even after slavery was abolished, Douglass kept fighting for equality. He argued for the importance of voting rights and other fair treatment for African Americans and women. Beginning in the early 1870s, he was appointed to several positions in the U.S. government. Among them were marshal in the District of Columbia and U.S. minister and consul general to Haiti. These positions made him the first African American to hold high rank in the government.

Douglass's meeting with Abraham Lincoln during the Civil War was just the start of his government leadership.

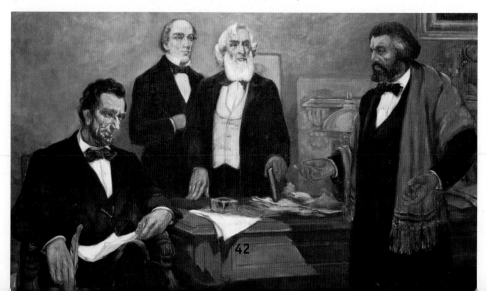

Douglass greets supporters after taking office as marshal of the District of Columbia.

Remembering a Hero

In 1895, at about the age of 77, Frederick Douglass died of heart failure. Around the world, people celebrated the life of this great man. With strength and determination, he had risen up from slavery to become one of the nation's most influential figures. He is remembered as a hero who fought bravely to end slavery and promote equality. His work continues to inspire people to this day. ★

Number of *North Star* subscribers at the height of the newspaper's popularity: About 4,000

Cost of a *North Star* subscription: $2 per year

Total number of enslaved people in the United States as of 1790: 697,897

Total number of enslaved people in the United States as of 1860: 3,953,760

Number of black soldiers who fought for the North during the Civil War: Around 180,000

Number of black soldiers who lost their lives fighting in the Civil War: Around 60,000

Did you find the truth?

T Frederick Douglass was the first African American to hold a high position in the U.S. government.

F Frederick Douglass's grandmother taught him how to read.

Resources

Books

Elliot, Henry. *Frederick Douglass: From Slavery to Statesman*. New York: Crabtree, 2010.

Ruffin, Frances E. *Frederick Douglass: Rising Up from Slavery*. New York: Sterling Publishing, 2008.

Stanley, George E. *Frederick Douglass: Abolitionist Hero*. New York: Simon & Schuster Books for Children, 2008.

Visit this Scholastic Web site for more information on Frederick Douglass:
★ www.factsfornow.scholastic.com
Enter the keywords **Frederick Douglass**

Important Words

abolitionist (ab-uh-LISH-uh-nist) — person who worked to end slavery permanently

activists (AK-ti-vists) — people who work for change

amendment (uh-MEND-muhnt) — a change that is made to a law or a legal document

autobiographies (aw-toh-bye-AH-gruh-feez) — books in which the author tells the story of his or her life

controversial (kahn-truh-VUR-shuhl) — causing a great deal of disagreement

depressed (di-PREST) — sad and unhappy with life

freedman (FREED-muhn) — a person who has been legally released from slavery

plantation (plan-TAY-shuhn) — a large farm where crops such as coffee, rubber, and cotton are grown

trough (TRAWF) — a long, narrow container that holds food or water and is traditionally used for animals; before the Civil War, it was sometimes used for feeding slaves

Underground Railroad (UHN-dur-ground RAYL-rode) — a network of people and places that helped slaves from the South escape to free states in the North or to Canada before the Civil War

Index

Page numbers in **bold** indicate illustrations.

abolitionists, 24, **25**, **28–29**, **30**, **32**, **34**, **35**, 37
Anthony, Captain, 9, 17
Auld, Hugh, 12, 14, 17, 22
Auld, Sophia, 13, 14, 15
Auld, Thomas, 12, 17, 18, 20
autobiographies, **31**, **41**

Bailey, Harriet (mother), 9
Baltimore, Maryland, 12, **15**, 17, **22**, 23
birth, 8, 40
Brown, John, **35**

childhood, **9**, 10–11, 12, 13, 14, 15
children, 27
Civil War, 40–41, **42**
Covey, Edward, 18–19

death, 43
dock work, **22**, 23, 25
Douglass, Anna (wife), **23**, 25, **26**, 27

education, **13**, **14**, 15, 20, 38
escape, 14, **21**, 22, 23, **24**, 25, 33, 35, 38, **40**
European travels, **32**, 33, 41

father, 9
Freeland, William, 20

Garrison, William Lloyd, **29**, **34**
government positions, 42, **43**

house laborers, **12**

Independence Day speech, 39

Lincoln, Abraham, **41**, **42**
London, England, **28**

marriage, 25

name, 8, 25, 40
Narrative of the Life of Frederick Douglass (autobiography), **31**, **41**
New Bedford, Massachusetts, 25, **26**, 27
New England Anti-Slavery Society, 29
newspapers, 15, 28, 34, 37, **38**
New York City, New York, 24, **25**
North Star, The (newspaper), 37, **38**

plantations, **8**, 10, **11**, 20, 40
punishments, **11**, 17, 18, **19**

Ruggles, David, 24, 25

slave breakers, **18**–19
speeches, 29, **30**, **32**, 35, 38, 39

13th Amendment, **41**
timeline, **40–41**
Truth, Sojourner, **35**
Tubman, Harriet, **35**

Underground Railroad, 35
U.S. Constitution, 41

voting rights, 42

Washington, D.C., 7, **41**, **42**
women's rights, 35, 38, 42
writings, **13**, 14, 15, **31**, 33, 38, **41**

About the Author

Josh Gregory has written more than 80 books covering a wide range of subjects. He lives in Chicago, Illinois.